Quotations
for
Successful
Living

"The wisdom of the wise and the experience
of the ages are perpetuated by quotations."

B. Disraeli

QUOTATIONS
FOR
SUCCESSFUL
LIVING

How to Live Life

collected and edited by
H.A. Levin

Abe Lincoln Press
New York

Abe Lincoln Press
58 Pasture Lane
Roslyn Heights, NY 11577

Publisher's Cataloging-in-Publication Data

Levin, Howard Alan.
Quotations for successful living: how to live life /
[collected and edited by] H.A. Levin.
Abe Lincoln Press:
Roslyn Heights, New York.
p. ; cm.
Includes index.
ISBN: 0-9636211-6-5
1. Conduct of life–Quotations, maxims, etc.
2. Quotations, American.   3. Quotations, English.
I. Levin, Howard Alan.

PN6084.L53H   1997
818'.5 DC20   97-072571

Manufactured in the United States of America

10 9 8 7 6 5 4 3 2 1

CONTENTS

QUOTATIONS ARE ARRANGED
BY AUTHORS' BIRTH DATES.

23rd Ave Staff,

*Dedicated
to
Your Success*

Be happy & healthy,
Friends Always,

Hal Leung 97

INTRODUCTION

As early as I can remember, our house was filled with how to live life quotations. They were posted on the refrigerator, kitchen cabinets, bathroom mirrors and other special places for the family to see. Many were clipped from magazines or newspapers, some were handwritten. Mom would put up new inspirational messages constantly, and she never threw the old ones away.

Instead, they grew into a collection and filled a box with positive thoughts on how others lived their lives. For as long as we remember them and what they said and how they lived, they still live in part through us. Twenty years ago the collection came into my possession. I continued to gather sayings and became curious about the lives of the authors who wrote them. I read what they wrote and what others wrote about them. The more I researched, the more I realized that those "great people" are more like you and me than they are different.

The negative and self-limiting voices that seem to creep and sometimes leap into my head are experienced by most everyone. Reading and rereading these quotes has helped me to replace negative thoughts with positive alternatives. I have learned to look for a rich and fulfilling life despite obstacles or fear of failure.

Reading deficiency is just one obstacle I had to overcome. Being dyslexic, I had a difficult time keeping up with my class. I was relegated to remedial classes. When I read how Helen Keller overcame being blind and deaf, my obstacles seemed to shrink by comparison. It helped to know that successful people had difficult days and seemingly impossible hurdles, yet they endured and prevailed.

My new found love of reading and my desire to make up for missed reading time prompted me to sell my television. Books are an essential part of my life and they have opened new and exciting avenues. Commercial sponsors might be happy to know that I bought a TV one year later, but the love of reading now is a way of life for me.

I have arranged the quotations chronologically by the authors' birth dates so it would give the reader a sense of history. Civilization has brought great technological advances, but the most important things in life remain the same.

My goal is to share these thoughts with as many people as possible.

H.A. Levin

"Our civilization is the sum of the knowledge and memories accumulated by generations that have gone before us. We can only partake of it if we are able to make contact with ideas of these past generations. The only way to do this – is by reading."

Anonymous

2500 B.C. – 1 B.C.

Following your desire as long as you live; do not lessen the time of following desire, for the wasting of time is an abomination to the spirit.

Ptahhotpe
b. 2350 B.C.

A journey of a thousand miles must begin with a single step.

Manifest plainness,
Embrace simplicity,
Reduce selfishness,
Have few desires.

The way of the sage is to act but not to compete.

Kindness in words creates confidence.
Kindness in thinking creates profoundness.
Kindness in giving creates love.

Lao-Tzu
b. 604 B.C.

There is no they, only us.

He who enjoys good health is rich, though he knows it not.

Anonymous

The nature of men is always the same; it is their habits that separate them.

Have no friends not equal to yourself.

The aim of the superior man is truth.

Silence is a true friend who never betrays.

What the superior man seeks is in himself.

To see what is right and not do it is lack of courage.

A youth is to be regarded with respect. How do you know that his future will not be equal to our present?

To be wronged is nothing unless you continue to remember it.

Confucius
b. 551 B.C.

Patience is the key to paradise.

Something can be sensed, not explained.

The truth is the safest lie.

Before enlightenment, chop wood, carry water. After enlightenment, chop wood, carry water.

Anonymous

No act of kindness, no matter how small, is ever wasted.

Appearances are often deceiving.

Don't count your chickens before they hatch.

United we stand, divided we fall.

Kindness effects more than severity.

Aesop
b. 550 B.C.

Everything flows, nothing stays still.

Nothing endures but change.

A man's character is his fate.

Heraclitus
b. 540 B.C.

Memory is the mother of all wisdom.

Old men are always young enough to learn, with profit.

Aeschylus
b. 525 B.C.

I will not steep my speech in lies; the test of any man lies in action.

Pindar
b. 518 B.C.

All men's gains are the fruits of venturing.

Mardonius
b. 5th century B.C.

Wonders are many, and none is more wonderful than man.

Ӝ

The greatest griefs are those we cause ourselves.

Ӝ

Truth ever has the most strength of what men say.

Ӝ

Wisdom outweighs any wealth.

Ӝ

Reason is God's crowning gift to man.

Ӝ

One word Frees us of all the weight and pain of life: That word is Love.

Ӝ

One must learn by doing the thing; though you think you know it, you have no certainty until you try.

Sophocles
b. 495 B.C.

Love is all we have, the only way that each can help the other.

Ӝ

Who so neglects learning in his youth, loses the past and is dead for the future.

Ӝ

Reason can wrestle and overthrow terror.

Ӝ

The company of just and righteous men is better than wealth and real estate.

Euripides
b. 485 B.C.

How many things can I do without!

∞

A life without inquiry is not worth living.

∞

I am a citizen, not of Athens or Greece, but of the world.

∞

Nothing can harm a good man, either in life or after death.

∞

Pay attention to the young, and make them just as good as possible.

∞

The greatest way to live with honor in this world is to be what we pretend to be.

Socrates
b. 469 B.C.

Life is short, art long, opportunity fleeting, experience treacherous, judgement difficult.

∞

The human soul develops up to the time of death.

∞

Healing is a matter of time, but it is sometimes also a matter of opportunity.

∞

Some patients, though conscious that their condition is perilous, recover their health simply through their contentment with the goodness of the physician.

Hippocrates
b. 460 B.C.

Every man is the architect of his own fortune.

Appius Claudis
b. 4th century B.C.

The beginning is half of the whole, and we all praise a good beginning.

∞

The direction in which education starts a man will determine his future life.

∞

If women are expected to do the same work as men, we must teach them the same things.

∞

A grateful mind is a great mind which eventually attracts to itself great things.

∞

No law or ordinance is mightier than understanding.

∞

Beauty of style and harmony and grace and good rhythm depend on simplicity.

∞

Truth is the beginning of every good thing, both in heaven and on earth; and he who would be blessed and happy should be from the first a partaker of truth, for then he can be trusted.

∞

The worst of all deceptions is self-deception.

Plato
b. 428 B.C.

Hope is a waking dream.

℅

All virtue is summed up in dealing justly.

℅

Happiness is at once the best, the noblest, and the pleasantest of things.

℅

Character is that which reveals moral purpose, exposing the class of things a man chooses or avoids.

℅

To be conscious that we are perceiving or thinking is to be conscious of our own existence.

℅

A plausible impossibility is always preferable to an unconvincing possibility.

Aristotle
b. 384 B.C.

To live is not to live for one's self alone; let us help one another.

Menander
b. 342 B.C.

A joy that's shared is a joy made double.

℅

Everything can change in a day.

℅

Give me fish, and I will eat for today; teach me to fish, and I will eat for the rest of my life.

Anonymous

No one knows what he can do till he tries.

∞

Anyone can steer the ship when the sea is calm.

∞

The timid way is safer, but they are slaves who take it.

∞

It's a bad plan that can't be changed.

∞

Never promise more than you can perform.

∞

While we stop to think, we often miss our opportunity.

∞

A good exterior is a silent recommendation.

∞

No man is happy who does not think himself happy.

Publilius Syrus
b. 1st century B.C.

My closest relation is myself.

Terence
b. 190 B.C.

Persistent kindness conquers the ill-disposed.

∞

Reason is the ruler and queen of all things.

∞

The people's good is the highest law.

∞

He does not seem to me to be a free man who does not sometimes do nothing.

Marcus Cicero
b. 106 B.C.

Every man's life lies within the present, for the past is spent and done with, and the future is uncertain.

Marcus Antonius
b. 83 B.C.

They are able because they think they are able.

Virgil
b. 70 B.C.

Who has self-confidence will lead the rest.

He who has begun has half done. Dare to be wise; begin!

Seize the day, and put the least possible trust in tomorrow.

The man who is tenacious of purpose in a rightful cause is not shaken from his firm resolve by the frenzy of his fellow citizens clamoring for what is wrong, or by the tyrant's threatening countenance.

Horace
b. 65 B.C.

Certain peace is better than anticipated victory.

Livy
b. 59 B.C.

Chance is always powerful. Let your hook be always cast. In the pool where you least expect it, will be a fish.

Ovid
b. 43 B.C.

A good man is always a beginner.

∞

Each day provides its own gifts.

∞

Tomorrow's life is too late. Live today.

Martial
b. 40 B.C.

Nature does not bestow virtue; to be good is an art.

∞

It is quality rather than quantity that matters.

∞

Economy is in itself a source of great revenue.

∞

Delight in teaching what you have learned.

∞

It is a rough road that leads to the heights of greatness.

∞

Let us train our minds to desire what the situation demands.

∞

If a man knows not what harbor he seeks, any wind is the right wind.

∞

There is nothing that Nature has made necessary which is more easy than death; we are longer a-coming into the world than going out of it; and there is not any minute of our lives wherein we may not reasonably expect it. Nay, it is but a moment's work, the parting of the soul and body. What a shame is it then to stand in fear of anything so long that is over so soon!

Lucius Seneca
b. 4 B.C.

1 A.D. – 1799

Only the educated are free.

∞

Only the just man enjoys peace of mind.

∞

It is difficulties that show what men are.

∞

The good or ill of man lies within his own will.

∞

First say to yourself what you would be; and then do what you have to do.

∞

On the occasion of every accident that befalls you, remember to turn to yourself and inquire what power you have for turning it to use.

Epictetus
b. 55

Fortune favors the bold.

∞

Revenge is the poor delight of little minds.

∞

Never does nature say one thing and wisdom another.

Juvenal
b. 60

The wealth of the soul is the only true wealth.

Lucian
b. 120

Our life is what our thoughts make it.

To live happily is an inward power of the soul.

Be neither the tyrant nor slave of any man.

Do every act of your life as if it were your last.

In a word, your life is short. You must make the most of the present with aid of reason and justice.

Since it is possible that you may be quitting life this very moment, govern every act and thought accordingly.

Marcus Aurelius
b. 121

Many receive advice, only the wise profit by it.

Ephraem Syrus
b. 308

There are some kinds of laughter that make you cry.

al-Mutnabbi
b. 915

Have patience. All things are difficult before they become easy.

Saadi
b. 1184

He who sees a need and waits to be asked for help is as unkind as if he had refused it.

Aligheri Dante
b. May 27, 1265

Thou, O God, dost sell us all good things at the price of labor.

Leonardo da Vinci
b. April 15, 1452

The most disadvantageous peace is better than the most just war.

Desiderius Eramus
b. October 27, 1465

I hope that I may desire more than I can accomplish.

Michelangelo
b. March 6, 1475

Everything that is done in the world is done by hope.

Martin Luther
b. November 10, 1483

Nothing is impossible to a willing heart.

∞

But in deed. A friend is never known till a man have need.

John Heywood
b. 1497

The ultimate in wisdom is to live in the present, plan for the future and profit from the past.

∞

Success satisfies but for a season; fame with a fearful finality; power passes with painful persistence; service to other abides without end.

Anonymous

There are defeats more triumphant than victories.

∞

Friendship is the highest degree of perfection in society.

∞

The value of life lies not in the length of days, but in the use we make of them; a man may live long yet live very little.

∞

If by being overstudious, we impair our health and spoil our good humor, let us give it up.

∞

We can be knowledgeable with other men's knowledge, but we cannot be wise with other men's wisdom.

∞

The man of understanding has lost nothing, if he has – if he owns – himself. The greatest thing in the world is to know how to be – to belong to – oneself.

Michel de Montaigne
b. February 28, 1533

Faint heart never won fair lady.

∞

A proverb is a short sentence based on long experience.

∞

Valor lies just halfway between rashness and cowardice.

∞

Make it thy business to know thyself, which is the most difficult lesson in the world.

Miguel de Cervantes
b. September 29, 1547

They are never alone that are accompanied with noble thoughts.

∞

In the performance of a good action, a man not only benefits himself, but he confers a blessing upon others.

Philip Sidney
b. November 30, 1554

Knowledge itself is power.

∞

Wise people make more opportunities than they find.

∞

Chiefly the mold of a man's fortune is in his own hands.

∞

In taking revenge, a man is but even with his enemy; but in passing it over, he is superior.

Francis Bacon
b. January 22, 1561

A closed mouth gathers no feet.

∞

If you don't know where you are going, any path will get you there.

∞

Knowing your strength makes you confident; forgetting your weakness makes you vulnerable.

Anonymous

Be not afraid of greatness.

∞

They do not love that do not show it.

∞

Our remedies oft in ourselves do lie.

∞

Virtue is bold, and goodness never fearful.

∞

The better part of valor is discretion.

∞

This above all: To thine own self be true.

∞

Everyone I meet is in some way my superior.

∞

One touch of nature makes the whole world kin.

∞

Most of what we think the world is doing to us, we are doing to ourselves.

∞

Our doubts are wantons, and make us lose the good we oft might win by fearing to attempt.

William Shakespeare
b. April 23, 1564

No man is an island entire of itself; every man is a part of the continent, a part of the main.

John Donne
b. 1572

He that would govern others first should be, the master of himself.

Philip Massinger
b. November 24, 1583

Good words are worth much, and cost little.

George Herbert
b. April 3, 1593

I think therefore I am.

Reading all the good books is like a conversation with the finest men of past centuries.

Rene Descartes
b. March 31, 1596

Help others solve their problems; standing farther away, you can often see matters more clearly than they do...The greatest service you can render someone else is helping him help himself.

Baltasar Gracian
b. 1601

Great hopes make great men.

He that travels much knows much.

Thomas Fuller
b. 1608

A true friend is the most precious of all possessions and the one we take the least thought about acquiring.

We all have enough strength to bear the misfortunes of others.

One is never as fortunate or as unfortunate as one imagines.

Francois La Rochefoucauld
b. September 15, 1613

Men of the noblest dispositions think themselves happiest when others share their happiness with them.

Jeremy Taylor
b. August 15, 1613

I bend but I do not break.

∞

Beware, as long as you live, of judging people by appearances.

Jean de La Fontaine
b. July 8, 1621

Things are only worth what you make them worth.

∞

The greater the obstacle, the more glory in overcoming it.

∞

Men are all alike in their promises. It is only in their deeds that they differ.

Moliere
b. 1622

Reading is to the mind what exercise is to the body.

Richard Steele
b. 1627

To love truth is the principal part of human perfection in this world, and the seed-plot of all others virtues.

∞

The thoughts that come unsought, and, as it were, drop into the mind, are commonly the most valuable of any we have.

John Locke
b. August 29, 1632

Wisdom sends us back to our childhood.

∞

We arrive at truth, not by reason only, but also by the heart.

Pascal
b. 1632

Most men that do thrive in the world do forget to take pleasure during the time that they are getting their estate, but reserve that till they have got one, and then it is too late for them to enjoy it.

Samuel Pepys
b. February 23, 1633

A man who is master of patience is master of everything else.

George Savile
b. November 11, 1633

Sense shines with a double luster when it is set in humility. An able man and yet humble man is a jewel worth a kingdom.

William Penn
b. October 14, 1644

There's none so blind as they that won't see.

∞

Vision is the art of seeing the invisible.

Jonathan Swift
b. November 30, 1667

Defer not till tomorrow to be wise, tomorrows sun to thee may never rise.

William Congreve
b. January 24, 1670

The hours of a wise man are lengthened by his ideas.

Joseph Addison
b. May 1, 1672

Procrastination is the thief of time.

Edward Young
b. 1683

To err is human, to forgive divine.

Do good by stealth, and blush to find it fame.

Charms strike the sight, but merit wins the soul.

Alexander Pope
b. May 21, 1688

Whatever is worth doing at all, is worth doing well.

Phillip Chesterfield
b. September 22, 1694

Life is thickly sown with thorns, and I know no other remedy than to pass quickly through them. The longer we dwell on our misfortunes, the greater is their power to harm us.

Four thousand volumes of metaphysics will not teach us what the soul is.

Voltarie
b. November 21, 1694

Any man who wants to succeed must begin by believing wholeheartedly in his own ability.

Anonymous

Eat to live, and not live to eat.

∞

The man who does things makes many mistakes but he never makes the biggest mistake of all – doing nothing.

∞

Dost thou love life? Then do not squander time, for that's the stuff life is made of.

∞

There never was a good war and a bad peace.

∞

Speak little; do much. Well done is better than well said.

∞

I want...to endeavor to speak truth in every instance; to give nobody expectations that are not likely to be answered, but aim at sincerity in every word and action – the most amiable excellence in a rational being.

∞

Being ignorant is not so much a shame as being unwilling to learn to do things the right way.

∞

If you would not be forgotten as soon as you are dead, either write things worth reading or do things worth writing.

Benjamin Franklin
b. January 17, 1706

There are few pleasures in the world so reasonable and so cheap as the pleasure of giving pleasure.

Anonymous

Clear your mind of can't.

∞

It matters not how a man dies, but how he lives.

∞

Few things in life are impossible to diligence and skill.

∞

Knowledge is of two kinds. We know a subject ourselves, or we know where we can find information upon it.

∞

If a man does not make new acquaintances as he advances through life, he will soon find himself alone.

∞

Self-confidence is the first requisite to great undertakings.

∞

It is better to live rich, than to die rich.

∞

Classical quotations are the parole of literary men all over the world.

Samuel Johnson
b. September 18, 1709

Every man has the right to risk his own life in order to save it.

Jean-Jacques Rousseau
b. 1712

Only passion, great passions, can elevate the soul to great things.

Denis Diderot
b. October 5, 1713

The busier we are, the more acutely we feel that we live, the more conscious we are of life.

Immanuel Kant
b. April 22, 1724

Labor to keep alive in your breast that little spark of celestial fire – conscience.

George Washington
b. February 22, 1732

Act well at the moment, and you have performed a good action for all eternity.

Johann K. Lavater
b. November 15, 1741

The most wasted of all days is that in which we have not laughed.

Sebastien Chamfort
b. 1741

I cannot live without books.

Delay is preferable to error.

It is neither wealth nor splendor, but tranquility and occupation, which give happiness.

When angry, count ten before you speak. If very angry, a hundred.

Nothing can stop the man with the right mental attitude from achieving his goal; nothing on earth can help the man with the wrong mental attitude.

Thomas Jefferson
b. April 13, 1743

Often the test of courage is not to die but to live.

Vittorio Alferi
b. January 16, 1749

What you can do, or dream you can do, Begin it, Boldness has genius, power and magic in it.

∞

Treat people as if they were what they ought to be and you help them become what they are capable of being.

∞

He is the happiest, be he king or peasant, who finds peace in his home.

∞

The deed is everything, the glory nothing.

∞

He who seizes the right moment, is the right man.

∞

The man who masters himself is delivered from the force that binds all creatures.

∞

Knowing is not enough, we must apply. Willing is not enough, we must do.

∞

Man errs as long as he strives.

Johann Wolfgang von Goethe
b. August 28, 1749

There's nothing so rewarding as to make people realize they are worthwhile in this world.

Robert Anderson
b. 1750

In idle wishes fools supinely stay, be there a will and wisdom finds a way.

George Crabbe
b. December 24, 1754

It is better to debate a question without settling it than to settle a question without debating it.

Joseph Joubert
b. 1754

Energy is eternal delight.

What is now proved was once only imagined.

He who knows not his own genius has none.

He whose face gives no light shall never be a star.

William Blake
b. November 28, 1757

Nature's mighty law is change.

Robert Burns
b. January 25, 1759

Only those who have the patience to do simple things perfectly will acquire the skill to do difficult things easily.

Johan von Schiller
b. November 10, 1759

Make happy those who are near and those who are far will come.

Anonymous

That best portion of a good man's life; His little, nameless, unremembered acts of kindness and of love.

∞

Wisdom is oft times nearer when we stoop than when we soar.

William Wordsworth
b. April 7, 1770

Conscience is but the pulse of reason.

Samuel T. Coleridge
b. October 21, 1772

We can do more good by being good than in any other way.

Rowland Hill
b. August 11, 1772

I shall pass through this world but once. If therefore there be any kindness I can show, or any good thing I can do, let me do it now; let me not deter it or neglect it.

Etienne de Grellet
b. 1773

The time will come when winter will ask what you were doing all summer.

Henry Clay
b. April 12, 1777

In order to profit from your mistakes, you have to get out and make some.

∞

He who thinks of others first should find the answers most easily.

Anonymous

Silence is the one great art of conversation.

If you think you can win, you can win. Faith is necessary to victory.

The least pain in our little finger gives more concern and uneasiness than the destruction of millions of our fellow beings.

William Hazlitt
b. April 10, 1778

Imitation is the sincerest flattery.

It is astonishing how much more anxious people are interested in lengthening life than improving it.

It is a common observation that any fool can get money; but they are not wise that think so.

Wealth, after all, is a relative thing, since he who has little, and wants less, is richer than he who has much and wants more.

Charles C. Colton
b. 1780

There is always room at the top.

Justice, sir, is the great interest of man on earth.

Daniel Webster
b. January 18, 1782

There is rapture on the lonely shore.

George Gordon Byron
b. January 22, 1788

Life is short, but truth works far and lives long; let us speak the truth.

Arthur Schopenhauer
b. 1788

The poetry of the earth is never dead.

John Keats
b. October 31, 1795

A man without a purpose is like a ship without a rudder.

∞

The greatest of faults, I should say, is to be conscious of none.

∞

The work an unknown good man has done is like a vein of water flowing hidden underground, secretly making the ground green.

Thomas Carlyle
b. December 4, 1795

If any man seeks for greatness, let him forget greatness and ask for truth, and he will find both.

Horace Mann
b. May 4, 1796

Life was not given for indolent contemplation and study of self, nor for brooding over emotions of piety: Action and actions only determine the worth.

Immanuel Fichte
b. July 18, 1797

Nothing contributes so much to tranquilizing the mind as a steady purpose – a point on which the soul may fix its intellectual eye.

Mary Wollstonecraft Shelley
b. August 30, 1797

1800 – 1899

Books are nothing but to inspire...Many times the reading of a book has made the fortune of the man – has decided his way of life.

All life is an experiment. The more experiments you make, the better.

A friend may well be reckoned the masterpiece of nature.

Criticism should not be querulous and wasting, but guiding, instructive, inspiring.

Every calamity is a spur and valuable hint.

A great man is always willing to be little.

You cannot do a kindness too soon because you never know how soon it will be too late.

Little minds have little worries, big minds have no time for worries.

Ralph Waldo Emerson
b. May 25, 1803

Beneath the rule of men entirely great, the pen is mightier than the sword.

Edward Lytton
b. 1803

Happiness is a butterfly, which, when pursued, is always just beyond your grasp, but which, if you sit down quietly, may alight upon you.

Nathaniel Hawthorne
b. July 4, 1804

Patience is a necessary ingredient of genius.

∞

The secret of success is constancy to purpose.

∞

Change is inevitable in a progressive society. Change is a constant.

∞

The secret of success in life is for a man to be ready for his opportunity when it comes.

∞

Action may not always bring happiness; but there is no happiness without action.

∞

What we anticipate seldom occurs; what we least expect generally happens.

∞

Next to knowing when to seize an opportunity, the most important thing in life is to know when to forego an advantage.

∞

The wisdom of the wise and the experience of the ages are perpetuated by quotations.

Benjamin Disraeli
b. December 21, 1804

The heart that loves is always young.

Anonymous

Light tomorrow with today.

Whoever loves true life, will love true love.

Elizabeth Barret Browning
b. March 6, 1806

Into each life some rain must fall, Some days must be dark and dreary.

Know how sublime a thing it is, to suffer and be strong.

Henry Wadsworth Longfellow
b. February 27, 1807

The highest possible stage in moral culture is when we recognize that we ought to control our thoughts.

Charles Darwin
b. February 12, 1809

Time is the only thing that can never be retrieved. One may lose and regain a friend; one may lose and regain money; opportunity that is once spurned may come again; but the hours that are lost in idleness can never be brought back to be used in gainful pursuits.

The giant oak is an acorn that held its ground.

Success thrives on giving more than on getting.

Anonymous

The best thing about the future is that it comes only one day at a time.

∞

What is conservatism? Is it not adherence to the old and tried, against the new and untried.

∞

Those who deny freedom to others, deserve it not for themselves.

∞

I am not concerned that you have fallen; I am concerned that you arise.

∞

It has been my experience that folks who have no vices have very few virtues.

∞

The sense of obligation to continue is present in all of us.

∞

It is true that you may fool all the people some of the time; you can even fool some of the people all the time; but you can't fool all of the people all the time.

∞

Truth is generally the best vindication against slander.

Abraham Lincoln
b. February 12, 1809

For man is man and master of his fate.

∞

Oh! yet we trust that somehow good will be the final goal of all.

Alfred Tennyson
b. August 6, 1809

A moment's insight is sometimes worth a life's experience.

∽

The mind, once expanded to the dimensions of larger ideas, never returns to its original size.

∽

It is a great deal better to be a self made man than not to be made at all.

∽

To be seventy years young is sometimes far more cheerful and hopeful than to be forty years old.

∽

How many men live on the reputation of the reputation they might have made.

Oliver Wendell Holmes, Jr.
b. August 29, 1809

The man who trusts men will make fewer mistakes than he who distrusts them.

Camillo Benso Cavour
b. August 10, 1810

When you get into a tight place and it seems you can't go on, hold on, for that's just the place and the time that the tide will turn.

Harriet Beecher Stowe
b. June 14, 1811

Take nothing on looks; take everything on evidence.

∽

I should never have made my success in life if I had not bestowed upon the last thing I have ever undertaken the same attention and care that I have bestowed upon the greatest.

Charles Dickens
b. February 7, 1812

Less is more.

∞

Ah, but a man's reach should exceed his grasp, Or what's a heaven for?

Robert Browning
b. May 7, 1812

Life can only be understood backwards, but must be lived forwards.

∞

To venture causes anxiety, but not to venture is to lose one's self...And to venture in the highest is precisely to become conscious of one's self.

Soren Kierkegaard
b. May 5, 1813

The ability to convert ideas to things is the secret of outward success.

Henry Ward Beecher
b. June 24, 1813

It takes a great man to be a good listener.

Arthur Helps
b. July 10, 1813

Nobody holds a good opinion of a man who has a low opinion of himself.

Anthony Trollope
b. April 24, 1815

We hold these truths to be self-evident, that all men and women are created equal...

Elizabeth Cady Stanton
b. November 12, 1815

Look twice before you leap.

Charlotte Bronte
b. April 21, 1816

In wildness is the preservation of the world.

As if you could kill time without injuring eternity.

Our life is frittered away by detail...Simplify, simplify.

That man is the richest whose pleasures are the cheapest.

Rather than love, than money, than fame, give me truth.

To regret deeply is to live afresh.

None are so old as those who have outlived enthusiasm.

I know of no more encouraging fact than the unquestionable ability of man to elevate his life by conscious endeavor.

Henry David Thoreau
b. July 12, 1817

There is no wealth but life.

When love and skill work together, expect a masterpiece.

John Ruskin
b. February 8, 1819

If you can't think up a new idea, try finding a way to make better use of an old idea.

Anonymous

Charity and personal force are the only investments worth anything.

Walt Whitman
b. May 31, 1819

Do noble things, do not dream them all day long.

Each man can learn something from his neighbor; at least he can learn to have patience with him – to live and let live.

Never, if possible, lie down at night without being able to say; I have made one human being, at least, a little wiser, a little happier, or a little better this day.

We act as though comfort and luxury were the chief requirement of life, when all that we need to make us really happy is something to be enthusiastic about.

Charles Kingsley
b. June 12, 1819

Our deeds determine us, as much as we determine our deeds.

Blessed is the man who, having nothing to say, abstains from giving in words evidence of the fact.

What do we live for, if it is not to make life less difficult for each other?

George Eliot (Mary Evans)
b. November 22, 1819

The queens in history compare favorably with the kings.

Men their rights and nothing more; women their rights and nothing less.

Join the union, girls, and together say, "Equal pay for equal work."

Woman must not depend upon the protection of man, but must be taught to protect herself.

Marriage, to woman as to man, must be a luxury, not a necessity; an incident of life, not all of it.

Susan B. Anthony
b. February 15, 1820

For what is done or learned by one class of women becomes, by virtue of their common womanhood, the property of all women.

Elizabeth Blackwell
b. February 3, 1821

It is not the brains that matter most, but that which guides them – the character, the heart, generous qualities, progressive ideas.

Fyodor Dostoyevski
b. November 11, 1821

The longer you live the more you realize that forgiveness, consideration and kindness are three of the great secrets in life.

Anonymous

Read in order to live.

∞

The most glorious moments in your life are not the so-called days of success, but rather those days when out of dejection and despair you feel rise in you a challenge of life, and then the promise of future accomplishments.

Gustave Flaubert
b. December 12, 1821

Everybody's business is nobody's business and nobody's business is my business.

Clara Barton
b. December 25, 1821

Genius is childhood recaptured.

Charles Baudelaire
b. 1821

Resolve to be thyself: and know that he who finds himself, loses his misery.

Matthew Arnold
b. December 24, 1822

Chance favors the prepared mind.

Louis Pastuer
b. December 27, 1822

Originality is simply a pair of fresh eyes.

Thomas W. Higgins
b. December 22, 1823

Whenever two ways lie before us, one of which is easy and the other hard, one of which requires no exertion while the other calls for resolution and endurance, happy is the person who chooses the mountain path and scorns the thought of resting in the valley. These are the men and women who are destined in the end to conquer and succeed.

Anonymous

There is the greatest practical benefit in making a few failures early in life.

∞

Perhaps the most valuable result of all education is the ability to make yourself do the thing you have to do, when it ought to be done, whether you like it or not.

∞

The great end of life is not knowledge but action.

Thomas Henry Huxley
b. May 4, 1825

The respect that is only bought by gold is not worth much.

Frances Harper
b. September 24, 1825

The brain is not, and cannot be, the sole or complete organ of thought and feeling.

Antoinette Brown Blackwell
b. 1825

The greatest pleasure in life is doing what people say that you cannot do.

Walter Bagehot
b. February 3, 1826

Be grateful for what you have, not regretful for what you haven't.

∞

Love is the great transformer, turning ambition into aspiration, selfishness into service, greed into gratitude, getting into giving and demands into dedication.

Anonymous

All, everything that I understand, I understand only because I love.

∞

Pure and complete sorrow is as impossible as pure and complete joy.

∞

It is amazing how complete is the delusion that beauty is goodness.

∞

Money is a new form of slavery, and distinguishable from the old simply by the fact that it is impersonal — that there is no human relation between master and slave.

Leo Tolstoy
b. August 28, 1828

He alone has lost the art to live who cannot win new friends.

S. Weir Mitchell
b. February 15, 1829

To live is so startling it leaves little time for anything else.

∞

We never know how high we are
    Till we are called to rise
    And then if we are true to plan
    Our statures touch the skies.

Emily Dickinson
b. December 10, 1830

To consider oneself different from ordinary men is wrong, but it is right to hope that one will not remain like ordinary men.

Yoshida Shoin
b. 1830

If wrinkles must be written upon our brows, let them not be written upon the heart. The spirit should not grow old.

James Garfield
b. November 19, 1831

Sometimes, I've believed as many as six impossible things before breakfast.

Lewis Carroll
b. January 27, 1832

Love is a great beautifier.

∞

Far away there in the sunshine are my highest aspirations. I can look up and see their beauty, believe in them, and try to follow where they lead.

∞

You have a good many little gifts and virtues, but there is no need of parading them, for conceit spoils the finest genius.

Louisa May Alcott
b. November 29, 1832

Justice is the only worship. Love is the only priest. Ignorance is the only slavery. Happiness is the only good. The place to be happy is here. The time to be happy is now. The way to be happy is to make others so.

Robert Ingersoll
b. August 11, 1833

You must capture and keep the heart of the original and supremely able man before his brain can do its best.

Andrew Carnegie
b. November 25, 1835

Life ain't no dress rehearsal!

∞

We are all alike, on the inside.

∞

A powerful agent is the right word. When in doubt, tell the truth.

∞

Few things are harder to put up with than a good example.

∞

The man who doesn't read good books has no advantage over the man who can't read them.

∞

Courage is resistance to fear, mastery of fear – not absence of fear.

∞

You can't depend on your eyes when your imagination is out of focus.

∞

We can secure other people's approval, if we do right and try hard; but our own is worth a hundred of it.

∞

Don't part with your illusions. When they are gone you may still exist, but you cease to live.

Samuel "Mark Twain" Clemens
b. November 30, 1835

Do not follow where the path may lead. Go instead where there is no path and leave a trail.

Anonymous

All animals, except man, know that the principal business of life is to enjoy it.

∞

The greatest pleasure of a dog is that you may make a fool of yourself with him and not only will he not scold you, but he will make a fool of himself too.

∞

The more lasting a man's ultimate work, the more sure he is to pass through a time, and perhaps a very long one, in which there seems to be very little hope for him.

Samuel Butler
b. December 4, 1835

As the valley gives height to the mountain, so can sorrow give meaning to pleasure; as the well is the source of the fountain, deep adversity can be a treasure.

∞

Greatness is not found in possessions, power, position or prestige. It is discovered in goodness, humility, service and character.

William Ward
b. 1835

If I were to name the three most precious resources of life, I should say books, friends, and nature; and the greatest of these, at least the most constant and always at hand, is nature.

John Burroughs
b. April 3, 1837

A man never sees all that his mother has been to him till it's too late to let her know that he sees it.

William Dean Howells
b. March 1, 1837

The clearest way into the universe is through a forest wilderness.

John Muir
b. July 21, 1838

They know enough who know how to learn.

Henry Brook Adams
b. February 16, 1839

To burn always with this hard gem-like flame, to maintain this ecstasy, is success in life.

Walter Pater
b. August 5, 1839

Be not afraid of life. Believe that life is worth living, and your belief will help create the fact.

∽

The greatest discovery of my generation is that human beings can alter their lives by altering their attitudes of mind.

∽

The great use of life is to spend it for something that will outlast it.

William James
b. January 11, 1842

The environment that people live in is the environment that they learn to live in, respond to, and perpetuate. If the environment is good, so be it. But if it is poor, so is the quality of life within it.

Ellen Swallow Richards
b. December 3, 1842

The right time is any time that one is still so lucky as to have...Live!

Henry James
b. 1843

One must never lose time in vainly regretting the past or in complaining against the changes which cause us discomfort, for change is the essence of life.

Anatole France
b. April 16, 1844

He who has a why to live can bear almost any how.

Fredrich Nietzsche
b. October 15, 1844

Life begets life. Energy creates energy. It is by spending oneself that one becomes rich.

Sarah Bernhardt
b. October 22, 1844

If you make fun of bad persons you make yourself beneath them.

Sarah Winnemucca
b. 1844

Everything comes to him who hustles while he waits.

Genius is one percent inspiration and ninety nine percent perspiration.

When down in the mouth, remember Jonah. He came out all right.

Our greatest weakness lies in giving up. The most certain way to succeed is to always try just one more time.

Thomas Alva Edison
b. February 11, 1847

When one door closes, another opens.

Alexander Graham Bell
b. March 3, 1847

I am the master of my fate; I am the captain of my soul.

William Henley
b. August 23, 1849

Two men look out through the same bars: One sees the mud, and one the stars.

Frederick Langbridge
b. 1849

You cannot run away from a weakness.

∞

To be feared of a thing and yet to do it, is what makes the prettiest kind of a man.

∞

Everyone lives by selling something.

∞

So long as we love we serve; so long as we are loved by others, I would almost say that we are indispensable; and no man is useless while he has a friend.

Robert Louis Stevenson
b. November 13, 1850

There are such wonderful possibilities in the life of each man and woman! No human being is unimportant. My inspiration comes in opening opportunities that all alike may be free to live life to the fullest.

Samuel Gompers
b. 1850

A successful man cannot realize how hard an unsuccessful man finds life.

Edgar Watson Howe
b. May 3, 1853

The best way to know God is to love many things.

Vincent Van Gogh
b. 1853

The supreme object of life is to live.

One's real life is so often the life that one does not lead.

To love oneself is the beginning of a life long romance.

Always forgive your enemies, nothing annoys them so much.

A dreamer is one who can only find his way by moonlight, and his punishment is that he sees the dawn before the rest of the world.

He knew the precise psychological moment when to say nothing.

I have the simplest tastes. I am always satisfied with the best.

Mistakes. Life would be dull without them.

Oscar Wilde
b. October 16, 1854

Anybody can be nobody, but it takes a man to be somebody.

Eugene V. Debs
b. November 5, 1855

Beauty is in the eye of the beholder.

Margaret Wolfe Hungerford
b. 1855

You can't hold a man down without staying down with him.

There is as much dignity in tilling a field as in writing a poem.

I learned that assistance given to the weak makes the one who gives it strong; and that oppression of the unfortunate makes one weak.

Booker T. Washington
b. April 5, 1856

Being entirely honest with oneself is a good exercise.

Sigmund Freud
b. May 6, 1856

If you would be interesting, be interested; if you would be pleased, be pleasing; if you would be loved, be lovable; if you would be helped be helpful.

He profits most who serves best.

Anonymous

You see things; and say, "Why?" But I dream things that never were; and say, "Why not?"

∞

People are always blaming their circumstances for what they are...The people who get on in this world are the people who get up and look for the circumstances they want, and, if they can't find them, make them.

∞

Imagination is the beginning of creation. You imagine what you desire; you will what you imagine; and at last you create what you will.

∞

We are all dependent on one another, every soul of us on earth.

∞

We have no more right to consume happiness without producing it than to consume wealth without producing it.

∞

A life spent making mistakes is not only more honorable but more useful than a life spent doing nothing.

∞

Life does not cease to be funny when people die any more than it ceases to be serious when people laugh.

∞

I want to be thoroughly used up when I die, for the harder I work the more I love. I rejoice in life for its own sake. Life is no brief candle to me; it is a sort of splendid torch which I've got a hold of for the moment and I want to make it burn as brightly as possible before handing it on to future generations.

George Bernard Shaw
b. July 26, 1856

We grow great by dreams. All big men are dreamers.

I not only use all the brains I have, but all I can borrow.

A fault which humbles a man is of more use to him than a good action which puffs him up.

Woodrow Wilson
b. December 28, 1856

The mind is capable of anything – because everything is in it, all the past as well as all the future.

I don't like work – no man does – but I like what is in work – the chance to find yourself. Your own reality – for yourself, not for others – what no other man can ever know.

Joseph Conrad
b. December 3, 1857

Do what you can, with what you have, with where you are.

I care not what others think of what I do, but I care very much about what I think of what I do. That is character.

The best executive is the one who has sense enough to pick good men to do what he wants done, and self-restraint enough to keep from meddling with them while they do it.

Theodore Roosevelt
b. October 27, 1858

There is no failure except in no longer trying.

∞

Do not take life too seriously. You will never get out of it alive.

∞

The world is moving so fast these days that the man who says it can't be done is generally interrupted by somebody doing it.

Elbert Hubbard
b. June 19, 1859

Education is a social process...Education is growth... Education is not preparation for life; education is life itself.

∞

Failure is instructive. The person who really thinks learns quite as much from his failures as from his successes.

∞

To find what one is fitted to do and to secure an opportunity to do it is the key to happiness.

John Dewey
b. October 20, 1859

Those who love deeply never grow old; they may die of old age, but they die young.

∞

He who allows his day to pass by without practicing generosity and enjoying life's pleasures is like a blacksmith's bellows – he breathes but does not live.

Anonymous

It is the close observation of little things which is the secret of success in business, in art, in science, and in every pursuit of life.

∞

The spirit of self-help is the root of all genuine growth in the individual; and, exhibited in the lives of many, it constitutes the true vigor and strength. Help from without is often enfeebling in its effects, but help from within invariably invigorates.

∞

We learn wisdom from failure much more than from success. We often discover what will do by finding out what will not do; and probably he who never made a mistake never made a discovery.

Samuel Smiles
b. 1859

Destiny is not a matter of chance, it is a matter of choice; it is not a thing to be waited for, it is a thing to be achieved.

William Jennings Bryan
b. March 19, 1860

Civilization is a method of living, an attitude of equal respect for all men.

Jane Addams
b. September 6, 1860

Happiness adds and multiplies as we divide it with others.

∞

We are continually faced by great opportunities brilliantly disguised as insoluble problems.

Anonymous

You can do anything if you have enthusiasm.

∞

Paying attention to simple little things that most men neglect makes a few men rich.

∞

But most people think of it in terms of getting; success, however, it begins in terms of giving.

∞

Failure is only the opportunity to begin again, more intelligently.

∞

The man who will use his skill and constructive imagination to how much he can give for a dollar, instead of how little he can give for a dollar, is bound to succeed.

∞

We want to live in the present, and the only history that is worth a tinker's damn is the history we make today.

∞

Let a man start out in life to build something better and sell it cheaper than it has been built or sold before, let him have that determination and the money will roll in.

Henry Ford
b. July 30, 1863

Those who cannot remember the past are condemned to repeat it.

∞

One's friends are that part of the human race with which one can be human.

George Santayana
b. December 16, 1863

The customer is always right.

Harry G. Selfridge
b. January 11, 1864

If you can meet with triumph and disaster and treat those two imposters just the same...

Rudyard Kipling
b. December 30, 1865

Had there been no difficulties and no thorns in the way, then man would have been in his primitive state and no progress made in civilization and mental culture.

Anabdabai Joshee
b. 1865

Prepare to live by all means, but for Heaven's sake do not forget to live.

Arnold Bennett
b. May 27, 1867

Nothing in life is to feared.
It is only to be understood.

∞

You cannot hope to build a better world without improving the individuals. To that end each of us must work for his own improvement, and at the same time share a general responsibility for all humanity, our particular duty being to aid those to whom we think we can be most useful.

Marie Curie
b. November 7, 1867

All things are to be examined and called into question. There are no limits set to thought.

Edith Hamilton
b. 1867

The return from your work must be the satisfaction which that work brings you and the world's need of that work. With this, life is heaven, or as near heaven as you can get. Without this – with work which you despise, which bores you, and which the world does not need – this life is hell.

William du Bois
b. 1868

He profits most who serves best.

A. F. Sheldon
b. 1868

A person cannot do right in one department whilst attempting to do wrong in another department. Life is one indivisible whole.

Mahatma Gandhi
b. October 2, 1869

One doesn't discover new lands without consenting to lose sight of the shore for a very long time.

∞

It is better to be hated for what you are than loved for what you are not.

Andre Gide
b. November 22, 1869

I'm a great believer in luck, and I find the harder I work the more I have of it.

Stephen Leacock
b. December 30, 1869

It is easier to fight for one's principles than to live up to them.

Alfred Adler
b. February 17, 1870

A great business success was probably never attained by chasing the dollar, but is due to pride in one's work, the pride that makes business an art.

Henry L. Doherty
b. May 15, 1870

From quiet homes and first beginning,
Out to discover ends,
There's nothing worth the wear of winning,
But laughter and the love of friends.

Hilaire Belloc
b. 1870

We are healed of suffering only by experiencing it to the fullest.

∞

In theory, one is aware that the earth revolves, but in practice one does not perceive it; the ground upon which one treads seems not to move, and one can live undisturbed. So it is with time in one's life.

Marcel Proust
b. July 10, 1871

The man who graduates today and stops learning tomorrow is uneducated the day after.

Newton D. Baker
b. December 3, 1871

Destiny is not a matter of chance, it's a matter of choice.

∞

Any man who lives to help other people will soon have other people living to help him.

Anonymous

Fear is the main source of superstition, and one of the main sources of cruelty. To conquer fear is the beginning of wisdom.

∞

If there were in the world today any large number of people who desire their own happiness more than they desired the unhappiness of others, we could have a paradise in a few years.

Bertrand Russell
b. May 18, 1872

No person was ever honored for what he received. Honor has been the reward for what he gave.

∞

I have never been hurt by anything I didn't say.

Calvin Coolidge
b. July 4, 1872

You will do foolish things, but do them with enthusiasm.

Sidonie Gabrielle Colette
b. January 28, 1873

Ah! The clock is always slow; it is later than you think.

Robert William Service
b. January 16, 1874

Great men are those who find that what they ought to do and want to do are the same thing.

∞

The most difficult thing in the world is to appreciate what we have – until we lose it.

Anonymous

There is only one thing about which I am certain, and that is that there is very little about which one can be certain.

∞

It is a funny thing about life; if you refuse to accept anything but the best, you very often get it.

∞

It wasn't until late in life that I discovered how easy it is to say, I don't know.

William Somerset Maugham
b. January 25, 1874

If one stands up and is counted, from time to time one may get knocked down. But remember this: a man flattened by an opponent can get up again. A man flattened by conformity stays down for good.

∞

It is a common mistake to think failure as the enemy of success. Failure is a teacher – a harsh one, but the best. Pull your failures to pieces looking for the reason. Put your failure to work for you.

Thomas J. Watson, Sr.
b. February 17, 1874

I shall be telling this with a sigh
Somewhere ages and ages hence;
Two roads diverged in a wood, and I,
I took the one less traveled by,
And that has made all the difference.

∞

Happiness makes up in height for what it lacks in length.

Robert Frost
b. March 26, 1874

No life is so hard that you can't make it easier by the way you take it.

Ellen Glasgow
b. April 27, 1874

There is a great man who makes every man feel small. But the real great man is the man who makes every man feel great.

∞

Where does a wise man kick a pebble? On the beach. Where does a wise man hide a leaf? In the forest.

Gilbert Chesterton
b. May 29, 1874

The price of greatness is responsibility.

∞

Courage is the first of human qualities because it is the quality which guarantees all the others.

∞

The quotations when engraved upon the memory give you good thoughts. They also make you anxious to read the authors and look for more.

∞

What is the use of living if it not be to strive for noble causes and to make this muddled world a better place for those who will live in it after we are gone?

Winston Churchill
b. November 30, 1874

Intuition is reason in a hurry.

Holbrook Jackson
b. December 31, 1874

Example is not the main thing in influencing others it is the only thing.

∞

Truth has no special time of its own. Its honor is now – always.

∞

I don't know what your destiny will be, but one thing I know: the only ones among you who will be really happy are those who will have sought and found how to serve.

Albert Schweitzer
b. January 14, 1875

Without this playing with fantasy no creative work has ever yet come to birth. The debt we owe to the play of imagination is incalculable.

Carl Gustav Jung
b. July 26, 1875

Count your garden by the flowers
Never by the leaves that fall;
Count your days by the golden hours,
Don't remember clouds at all.
Count the nights by stars, not shadows,
Count your life by smiles, not tears,
And with joy on every birthday
Count your age by friends, not years.

∞

If you do not believe in yourself, very few other people will.

Anonymous

Learn how to fail intelligently.

∞

We should all be concerned about the future because we will have to spend the rest of our lives there.

∞

There is a great difference between knowing a thing and understanding it, you can know a lot and not really understand anything.

∞

Every great improvement – has come after repeated failures. Virtually nothing comes out right the first time. Failures, repeated failures, are finger posts on the road to achievement.

∞

Keep on going and the chances are you will stumble on something, perhaps when you are least expecting it.

∞

No one ever would have crossed the ocean if he could have gotten off the ship in the storm.

∞

A man must have a certain amount of intelligent ignorance to get anywhere.

Charles F. Kettering
b. August 29, 1876

For loneliness is but cutting adrift from our moorings and floating out to the open sea; an opportunity for finding ourselves, our real selves, what we are about, where we are heading during our little time on this beautiful earth.

Anne Shannon Monroe
b. 1877

Imagination is more important than knowledge.

∞

Everything should be made as simple as possible, but not simpler.

∞

The most beautiful thing we can experience is the mysterious. It is the source of all true art and science.

∞

Physical concepts are free creations of the human mind, and are not, however it may seem, uniquely determined by the external world.

∞

I would ask them to spend an hour everyday rejecting the ideas of others and thinking things out for themselves. This will be a hard thing to do but it will be rewarding.

∞

Every kind of peaceful cooperation among men is primarily based on mutual trust and only secondarily on institutions such as courts of justice and police.

∞

Peace cannot be kept by force. It can only be achieved by understanding.

∞

I think and think for months and years. Ninety-nine times, the conclusion is false. The hundreth time I am right.

Albert Einstien
b. March 14, 1879

The optimist proclaims that we live in the best of all possible worlds; and the pessimist fears this is true.

James Branch Cabell
b. April 14, 1879

You grow up the day you have the first real laugh – at yourself.

∞

You must learn day by day, year by year to broaden your horizon. The more things you love, the more you are interested in, the more you enjoy, the more you are indignant about – the more you have left when anything happens.

Ethel Barrymore
b. August 15, 1879

Even if you're on the right track, you'll get run over if you just sit there.

Will Rogers
b. November 4, 1879

Start every day off with a smile and get it over with.

W. C. Fields
b. April 9, 1880

Large-scale success today is spelled – Teamwork.

∞

The things that are most worthwhile in life are really those within the reach of almost every normal human being who cares to seek them out.

Charles B. Forbes
b. May 14, 1880

Literature is my utopia.

∞

Face your deficiencies and acknowledge them. But do not let them master you.

∞

Keep your face to the sunshine and you cannot see the shadow.

∞

There is no king who has not had a slave among his ancestors, and no slave who has not had a king among his.

∞

The highest result of education is tolerance.

∞

One can never consent to creep when one feels an impulse to soar.

∞

It gives me a deep, comforting sense that things seen are temporal and things unseen are eternal.

∞

Security is mostly a superstition... Avoiding danger is no safer in the long run than outright exposure. Life is either a daring adventure or nothing.

Helen Adams Keller
b. June 27, 1880

You come into the world with nothing, and the purpose of your life is to make something out of nothing.

Henry Louis Mencken
b. September 12, 1880

For when the One Great Scorer comes
To mark against your name,
He writes – not that you won or lost
But how you played the game.

Grantland Rice
b. November 1, 1880

Most of us serve our ideas by fits and starts. The person who makes a success of living is the one who sees his goal steadily and aims for it unswerving.

Cecil B. De Mille
b. August 12, 1881

Computers are useless. They can only give you answers.

Pablo Picasso
b. October 25, 1881

Peace, like charity, begins at home.

∞

Physical strength can never permanently withstand the impact of spiritual force.

∞

It is common sense to take a method and try it. If it fails, admit it frankly and try another. But above all, try something.

∞

People acting together as a group can accomplish things which no individual acting alone could ever hope to bring about.

∞

Happiness lies in the joy of achievement and the thrill of creative effort.

∞

When you get to the end of your rope, tie a knot and hang on.

Franklin Delano Roosevelt
b. January 30, 1882

No man can think clearly when his fists are clenched.

George Jean Nathan
b. February 14, 1882

Problems are only opportunities in work clothes.

∞

When your work speaks for itself, don't interrupt.

Henry J. Kaiser
b. May 4, 1882

In the long run...we are all dead.

John Maynard Keynes
b. June 5, 1883

How many cares one loses when one decides not to be something but to be someone.

Gabrielle "Coco" Chanel
b. August 19, 1883

It is well to give when asked, but it is better to give unasked.

Kahil Gibran
b. 1883

The successful man has enthusiasm.

∞

Every great achievement is the story of a flaming heart.

∞

A pessimist is one who makes difficulties of his opportunities; an optimist is one who makes opportunities of his difficulties.

Harry Truman
b. May 8, 1884

It is better to light a candle than to curse the darkness.

∞

Life was meant to be lived, and curiosity must be kept alive.

∞

No one can make you feel inferior without your consent.

∞

You must do the thing you think you cannot do.

∞

It is not fair to ask of others what you are not willing to do yourself.

∞

The future belongs to those who believe in the beauty of their dreams.

∞

It isn't enough to talk about peace. One must believe in it. And it isn't enough to believe in it. One must work at it.

∞

When you cease to make a contribution you begin to die.

Eleanor Roosevelt
b. October 11, 1884

Take calculated risks. This is quite different from being rash.

George S. Patton
b. November 11, 1885

Properly we should read for power. Man reading should be man intensely alive. The book should be a ball of light in one's hand.

Ezra Pound
b. 1885

Go around asking a lot of damn fool questions and taking chances. Only through curiosity can we discover opportunities, and only by gambling can we take advantage of them.

Clarence Birdseye
b. December 9, 1886

Many of us spend half our time wishing for things we could have if we didn't spend half our time wishing.

Alexander Woollcott
b. January 19, 1887

A closed mind is a dying mind.

Edna Ferber
b. August 15, 1887

Generosity is giving what you could use yourself.

Marianne Moore
b. November 15, 1887

When you give away some of the light from the candle, by lighting another person's candle there isn't less light because you've given some away – there's more. That works with love too.

∞

He that can't endure the bad will not live to see the good.

∞

Abilities not used are wasted.

Anonymous

Take a chance! All life is a chance.

∞

When dealing with people, let us remember we are not dealing with creatures of logic. We are dealing with creatures of emotion, creatures bristling with prejudices and motivated by pride and vanity.

∞

You can make more friends in two months by becoming really interested in other people than you can in two years by trying to get other people interested in you.

∞

There is only one way under high Heaven to get anybody to do anything. Did you ever stop to think of that? Yes, just one way. And that is by making the other person want to do it.

Dale Carnegie
b. November 24, 1888

Make it a rule of life never to regret and never to look back. Regret is an appalling waste of energy; you can't build on it; it's only good for wallowing in.

Katherine Mansfield
b. 1888

The basic fact of today is the tremendous pace of change in human life.

Jawaharlal Nehru
b. November 14, 1889

There is only one success – to be able to spend your life in your own way.

∞

Read every day something no one else is reading. Think something no one else is thinking. It is bad for the mind to be always a part of unanimity.

Christopher Morley
b. May 5, 1890

Deliberation is the work of many men. Action, of one alone.

Charles de Gaulle
b. November 22, 1890

Courage is doing what you're afraid to do. There can be no courage unless you're scared.

Eddie Rickenbacker
b. 1890

Let the world know you as you are, not as you think you should be, because sooner or later, if you are posing, you will forget the pose, and then where are you?

Fannie Brice
b. October 29, 1891

No country can advance unless its women advance.

Marie Casey
b. 1891

Not truth, but faith, it is that keeps the world alive.

Edna St. Vincent Millay
b. February 22, 1892

One faces the future with one's past.

Pearl Buck
b. 1892

He who hesitates is a damned fool.

∞

It's not the men in my life that counts, it's the life in my men.

Mae West
b. August 17, 1892

Humor is a prelude to faith and laughter is the beginning of prayer.

Reinhold Niebuhr
b. 1892

If you have made mistakes, even serious ones, there is always another chance for you. What we call failure is not the falling down, but the staying down.

Mary Pickford
b. April 8, 1893

If we want a thing badly enough, we make it happen. If we let ourselves be discouraged, that is proof that our wanting was inadequate.

Dorothy Sayers
b. June 13, 1893

The future comes one day at a time.

Dean Acheson
b. 1893

Dance is the hidden language of the soul.

Martha Graham
b. May 11, 1894

Everyone should take an interest in the future – that's where you will spend the rest of your life.

Anonymous

Courage, it would seem, is nothing less than the power to overcome danger, misfortune, fear, injustice, while continuing to affirm inwardly that life with all its sorrows and good is meaningful even if in a sense beyond our understanding, and that there is always tomorrow.

Dorothy Thompson
b. July 9, 1894

There is only one corner of the universe you can be certain of improving, and that's your own self.

∞

Facts do not cease to exist because they are ignored.

Aldous Leonard Huxley
b. July 26, 1894

A part of control is learning to correct your weaknesses. The person doesn't live who was born with everything.

∞

You just can't beat the person who never gives up.

George "Babe" Ruth
b. February 6, 1895

Dare to be naive.

∞

Don't fight forces; use them.

Buckminster Fuller
b. February 12, 1895

I was always looking outside myself for strength and confidence but it comes from within. It is there all the time.

Anna Freud
b. December 3, 1895

The dinosaur's eloquent lesson is that if some bigness is good, an overabundance of bigness is not necessarily better.

Eric A. Johnston
b. 1895

Sometimes it is more important to discover what one cannot do, than what one can do.

Lin Yutang
b. 1895

I'd rather be a failure at something I enjoy than be a success at something I hate.

George Burns
b. January 20, 1896

A hairline separates people who make good and people who don't – and those who make it should help the ones who don't, because they are the custodians of worldly goods, not the owners.

Jay Phillips
b. March 22, 1896

Whatever women do they must do twice as well as men to be thought half as good. Luckily, this is not difficult.

Charlotte Whitton
b. May 31, 1896

A person does things for the sake of accomplishing something. Money generally follows.

Henry Crown
b. 1896

Tact is a priceless quality in good human relations.

Donald A. Laird
b. May 14, 1897

You cannot shake hands with a clenched fist.

∞

Those who do not know how to weep with their whole heart don't know how to laugh either.

Golda Meir
b. May 3, 1898

Adventure is worthwhile in itself.

∞

Courage is the price that life exacts for granting peace. The soul that knows it not, knows no release from little things; knows not the livid loneliness of fear, nor mountain heights where bitter joy can hear, the sound of wings.

Amelia Earhart
b. July 24, 1898

To love at all is to be vulnerable.

Clive S. Lewis
b. 1898

Never mistake motion for action.

∞

Time is the least thing we have of.

∞

Do not reverse a decision out of fear alone.

∞

Now is no time to think of what you do not have. Think of what you can do with what there is.

Ernest Hemingway
b. July 21, 1899

1900 – Present

Man's main task in life is to give birth to himself.
Erich Fromm
b. March 23, 1900

Life's under no obligation to give us what we expect. We take what we get and are thankful it's no worse than it is.
Margaret Mitchell
b. November 8, 1900

Perfection is finally attained, not when there is no longer anything to add, but when there is no longer anything to take away.
Antoine de Saint-Exupery
b. 1900

An expert is someone who knows some of the worst mistakes that can be made in his subject, and how to avoid them.
Werner Heisenberg
b. December 5, 1901

If we are to achieve a richer culture, rich in contrasting values, we must recognize the whole gamut of human potentialities, and so weave a less arbitrary social fabric, one in which each diverse human gift will find a fitting place.

We are living beyond our means. As a people we have developed a life-style that is draining the earth of its priceless and irreplaceable resources without regard for the future of our children and people all around the world.
Margaret Mead
b. December 16, 1901

It's the friends you can call up at 4 A.M. that matter.

Marlene Dietrich
b. December 27, 1901

As long as you keep a person down, some part of you has to be down there to hold him down, so it means you cannot soar as you otherwise might.

Marian Anderson
b. February 17, 1902

If you don't want to work, you have to work to earn enough money so that you won't have to work.

Ogden Nash
b. August 19, 1902

It's a matter of having principles. It's easy to have principles when you're rich. The important thing is to have principles when you're poor.

Ray A. Kroc
b. October 5, 1902

We don't see things as they are, we see them as we are.

∞

Each friend represents a world in us, a world possibly not born until they arrive, and it is only by this meeting that a new world is born.

∞

There are very few human beings who receive the truth, complete and staggering, by instant illumination. Most of us acquire it fragment by fragment, on a small scale, by successively, cellularly, like a laborious mosaic.

∞

People living deeply have no fear of death.

Anais Nin
b. February 21, 1903

Never forget that only dead fish swim with the stream.

Malcolm Muggeridge
b. March 24, 1903

Love has pride in nothing – but its own humility.

Clare Boothe Luce
b. April 10, 1903

I'm fat, but I'm thin inside. Has it ever struck you that there's a thin man inside every fat man, just as they say there's a statue inside every block of stone?

George Orwell
b. June 25, 1903

Few people recognize opportunity, because it comes disguised as hard work.

Cary Grant
b. January 18, 1904

A failure is not always a mistake; it may simply be the best one can do under the circumstances. The real mistake is to stop trying.

B. F. Skinner
b. March 20, 1904

If you achieve success, you will get applause, and if you get applause you will hear it. My advice to you concerning applause is this; enjoy it, but never quite believe it.

Robert Montgomery
b. May 21, 1904

A teacher for one day is like a parent for a lifetime.

Anonymous

You can have anything you want if you make up
your mind and you want it.*

Clara McBride Hale
b. April 1, 1905

How old would you be, if you didn't know how old
you was?

Satchel Paige
b. August 6, 1905

The world is round and the place which may seem
like the end, may also be only the beginning.

Ivy Baker Priest
b. September 7, 1905

It's not what they do to you, it's what you do with
what they do to you, that counts.

Jean-Paul Sartre
b. 1905

Don't let life discourage you; everyone who got where
he is had to begin where he was.

Richard L. Evans
b. March 23, 1906

Forgiveness is the key to action and freedom.

Hannah Arendt
b. October 4, 1906

Whoever you are, there is some younger person who
thinks you are perfect. There is some work that will
never be done if you don't do it. There is someone who
would miss you if you are gone. There is a good reason
for becoming better than you are. There is a place
that you alone can fill.

Anonymous

No moral man can have peace of mind if he leaves undone what he knows he should have done.

Tomorrow is the most important thing in life. Comes in to us at midnight very clean. It's perfect when it arrives and it puts itself in our hands and hopes we've learned something from yesterday.

John Wayne
b. May 26, 1907

It takes as much courage to have tried and failed as it does to have tried and succeeded.

Anne Morrow Lindbergh
b. June 22, 1907

Above all, do not talk yourself out of good ideas by trying to expound them at haphazard meetings.

Jacques Barzun
b. November 30, 1907

If we really want to live, we'd better start at once to try; If we don't, it doesn't matter, we'd better start to die.

Wystan Hugh Auden
b. 1907

Doing business without advertising is like winking at a girl in the dark. You know what you are doing, but nobody else does.

Stewart Henderson Britt
b. June 17, 1907

One is not born a woman, one becomes one.

Simone de Beauvoir
b. January 9, 1908

We have to understand the world can only be grasped by action, not by contemplation.

Jacob Bronowski
b. January 18, 1908

Just because your voice reaches halfway around the world doesn't mean you are wiser than when it reached only to the end of the bar.

Edward R. Murrow
b. April 25, 1908

You have to develop a style that suits you and pursue it, not just develop a bag of tricks. Always be yourself.

Jimmy Stewart
b. May 20, 1908

There's something special for everyone to do. Remember, no experience is a bad experience unless you gain nothing from it.

Lyndon Baines Johnson
b. August 27, 1908

Men can starve from a lack of self-realization as much as they can from lack of bread.

Richard Wright
b. September 4, 1908

Faced with the choice between changing one's mind and proving there is no need to do so, almost everyone gets busy on the proof.

John Kenneth Galbraith
b. October 15, 1908

Success is that old ABC – ability, breaks and courage.

Charles Luckman
b. May 16, 1909

I think living is an adventure.

∞

Without discipline, there's no life at all.

∞

To keep your character intact you cannot stoop to filthy acts. It makes it easier to stoop the next time.

Katharine Hepburn
b. November 8, 1909

Plans are worthless, but planning is invaluable.

∞

Whenever you see a successful business, someone once made a courageous decision.

Peter F. Drucker
b. November 9, 1909

We can do no great things, only small things with great love.

∞

Loneliness and the feeling of being unwanted is the most terrible poverty.

∞

Kind words can be short and easy to speak, but their echoes are truly endless.

Mother Teresa
b. August 27, 1910

Be more concerned with your character than your reputation, because your character is what you really are, while your reputation is merely what others think you are.

John Wooden
b. October 14, 1910

Life is all memory except for the one present moment that goes by so quick you can hardly catch it going by.

Tennessee Williams
b. March 26, 1911

I have an everyday religion that works for me: Love yourself first and everything else falls into line. You really have to love yourself to get anything done in this world.

Lucille Ball
b. August 6, 1911

I just sat down and started all by myself. It never occurred to me that I couldn't do it as well as anybody.

∽

When people don't have an objective there's much less dynamic effort and that makes life a lot less interesting.

Barbara Tuchman
b. January 30, 1912

Humor is the best therapy.

∽

The eternal quest of the individual human being is to shatter his loneliness.

Norman Cousins
b. June 24, 1912

We've got to work to save our children and do it
with the full respect for the fact that if we do not, no
one else is going to do it.

Dorothy Irene Height
b. 1912

What we are is God's gift to us. What we become is
our gift to God.

Eleanor Powell
b. 1912

You can't give people pride, but you can provide the
kind of understanding that makes people look to their
inner strengths and find their own sense of pride.

Charleszetta Waddles
b. 1912

Life is a great big canvas, and you should throw all
the paint on it you can.

Danny Kaye
b. January 18, 1913

Winning isn't everything, but wanting to win is.

∞

Individual commitment to a group effort – that is
what makes a team work, a company work, a society
work, a civilization work.

Vince T. Lombardi
b. June 11, 1913

You can stay alive as long as you live by keeping
your mind alert, by feeding yourself new ideas, by
exploring the world of ideas with the help of the books
in your own public library.

Anonymous

You must prepare for your future and that is the key to education.

∞

When you make a mistake, there are only three things you should ever do about it: admit it; learn from it, and don't repeat it.

Paul "Bear" Bryant
b. September 11, 1913

To know oneself, one should assert oneself.

∞

In the mist of winter, I finally learned that there was in me an invincible summer.

Albert Camus
b. November 7, 1913

Do not go gentle into that good night,
Old age should burn and rave at close of day;
Rage, rage against the dying of the light.

Dylan Thomas
b. October 27, 1914

A person always doing his or her best becomes a natural leader, just by example.

∞

If you keep thinking about what you want to do or what you hope will happen, you don't do it, and it won't happen.

Joe DiMaggio
b. November 24, 1914

With every dollar you save a dime, you spend a quarter or fifty cents, and you give some of it away. To me, that's a spiritual use of money.*

Margaret Walker Alexander
b. July 7, 1915

I've never sought success in order to get fame and money; it's the talent and the passion that count in success.

Ingrid Bergman
b. August 15, 1915

Good instincts usually tell you what to do long before your head has figured it out.

Michael Burke
b. August 6, 1916

Being courageous requires no exceptional qualifications, no magic formula, no special combination of time, place and circumstance.
It is an opportunity that sooner or later is presented to us all.

∽

Our privileges can be no greater than our obligations. The protection of our rights can endure no longer than the performance of our responsibilities.

John Fitzgerald Kennedy
b. May 29, 1917

I didn't want to write about somebody who turned out to be a star 'cause most people don't turn out to be stars. And yet their lives are just as sweet and just as rich as any others and often they are richer and sweeter.

Gwendolyn Brooks
b. June 7, 1917

Don't be afraid to feel as angry or as loving as you can, because when you feel nothing, it's just death.*

Lena Horne
b. June 30, 1917

Never go to bed mad. Stay up and fight.

∞

I've been broke but I've never been poor.

Phyllis Diller
b. July 17, 1917

The most important thing is to be a survivor, to stick it out through thick and thin.

Reid Anderson
b. 1917

Love from one being to another can only be that two solitudes come nearer, recognize and protect and comfort each other.

Han Suyin
b. 1917

I think that is Number 1 – the ability to handle uncertainty.

David A. Thomas
b. 1917

Everybody wants to do something to help, but nobody wants to be first.

Pearl Bailey
b. March 29, 1918

Expect trouble as an inevitable part of life and repeat to yourself, the most comforting words of all; This, too, shall pass.

Ann Landers
b. July 4, 1918

A life is not important except the impact it has on others.

Jackie Robinson
b. January 31, 1919

The one important thing I have learned over the years is the difference between taking one's work seriously and taking one's self seriously. The first is imperative and the second is disastrous.

Margot Fonteyn
b. May 18, 1919

You don't have to be a fantastic hero to do certain things...You can be an ordinary chap, sufficiently motivated to reach challenging goals. The intense effort, the giving of everything you've got is a very pleasant bonus.

Edmund Hillary
b. July 20, 1919

Honesty is the corner stone of character.

∞

There is no joy which surpasses that which springs from consciousness of work well done...

∞

One worthwhile task carried to a successful conclusion is worth half-a-hundred half-finished tasks.

∞

A word of appreciation often can accomplish what nothing else could accomplish.

Malcolm Forbes
b. August 19, 1919

Think wrongly, if you please, but in all cases think for yourself.

∞

There is only one real sin and that is to persuade oneself that the second-best, is anything but second best.

Doris Lessing
b. October 22, 1919

It's almost not necessary for us to do good; it's only necessary for us to stop doing evil, for goodness sake.

Isaac Asimov
b. January 2, 1920

Trouble is a part of life, and if you don't share it, you don't give the person who loves you a chance to love you enough.

Dinah Shore
b. March 1, 1920

Stand for something. Don't quest for popularity at the expense of morality and ethics and honesty.

Howard Cosell
b. March 25, 1920

You always pass failure on the way to success.

Mickey Rooney
b. September 23, 1920

What once was thought can never be undone.

Friedrich Durrenmatt
b. January 5, 1921

We cannot expect in the immediate future that all women who seek it will achieve full equality of opportunity. But if women are to start moving towards that goal, we must match our aspirations with the competence, courage and determination to succeed.

Roslyn Sussman Yalow
b. July 19, 1921

Something which we think is impossible now is not impossible in another decade.*

∽

You can't invent events. They just happen. But you have to be prepared to deal with them when they happen.*

Constance Baker Motley
b. 1921

Success is what you do with the ability that you have, how you use your talent. It doesn't necessarily mean any one thing.

George Allen
b. April 29, 1922

The individual can make a difference.*

Rachel Robinson
b. July 19, 1922

I wasn't afraid to fail. Something good always comes out of failure.

Ann Baxter
b. May 7, 1923

You do a lot of things, sometimes, before you can decide what you want to do.*

Georgia Davis Powers
b. October 19, 1923

Leadership is a matter of having people look at you and gain confidence by seeing how you react. If you're in control, they're in control.

Tom Landry
b. September, 11, 1924

Service is the rent that you pay for room on this earth.*

Shirley Chisholm
b. November 30, 1924

It's always been 10 percent talent and 90 percent hard work.

Paul Newman
b. January 26, 1925

The game isn't over till it's over.

Lawrence "Yogi" Berra
b. May 12, 1925

Early in life, I had learned that if you want something, you had better make some noise.

No man has believed perfectly until he wishes for his brother what he wishes for himself.

Truly a paradise could exist wherever material progress and spiritual values could be properly balanced.

In all our deeds, the proper value and respect for time determines success or failure.

I think that anybody who is in a position to discipline others should first learn to accept discipline himself.

Malcolm X
b. May 19, 1925

You may have to fight a battle more than once to win it.

Margaret Thatcher
b. October 13, 1925

There are long periods when life seems a small, dull round, a petty business with no point, and then suddenly we are caught up in some great event which gives us a glimpse of the solid and durable foundations of our existence.

Elizabeth II
b. April 21, 1926

When people look only at the surface and that satisfies them and they think from that surface they see, that is to be truly blind.*

Beah Richards
b. July 12, 1926

Success is never final; failure is never fatal.

You've got to believe deep inside yourself that you're destined to do great things.

Joe Paterno
b. December 21, 1926

The one thing that doesn't abide by majority rule is a person's conscience.

Until I feared I would lose it, I never loved to read. One does not love breathing.

Harper Lee
b. April 26, 1926

The ultimate lesson all of us have to learn is unconditional love, which includes not only others but ourselves as well.

Elizabeth Kubler-Ross
b. 1926

Accomplishments have no color.

∞

You should always know when you're shifting gears in life. You should leave your era, it should never leave you.*

Leontyne Price
b. February 10, 1927

I think the way I want to think. I live the way I want to live.

Sidney Poitier
b. February 20, 1927

The difference between the impossible and the possible lies in a person's determination.

Tommy Lasorda
b. September 22, 1927

The only place where success comes before work is in a dictionary.

Vidal Sassoon
b. January 17, 1928

Familiarity, truly cultivated, can breed love.

∞

Trust your hunches. They're usually based on facts filed away just below the conscious level.

∞

Anger repressed can poison a relationship as surely as the cruelest words.

∞

A strong, positive self-image is the best possible preparation for success in life.

Joyce Brothers
b. October 20, 1928

The world has improved mostly through people who
are unorthodox, who do unorthodox things.*

Ruby Dee
b. October 27, 1928

Nobody can teach you how to sing the blues, you
have to feel the blues.

Ernestine Anderson
b. 1928

The time is always right to do what is right.

Injustice anywhere is a threat to justice everywhere.

We must accept finite disappointment, but we must
never lose infinite hope.

All progress is precarious, and the solution of one
problem brings us face to face with another problem.

That old law about "an eye for an eye" leaves
everybody blind.

Man must evolve for all human conflict a method
which rejects revenge, aggression and retaliation. The
foundation of such a method is love.

Martin Luther King, Jr.
b. January 15, 1929

The man who graduates today and stops learning
tomorrow is uneducated the day after.

Anonymous

There are no shortcuts to any place worth going.

∞

You may be disappointed if you fail, but you are doomed if you don't try.

Beverly Sills
b. May 25, 1929

Think of all the beauty still left around you and be happy.

∞

In spite of everything I still believe that people are really good at heart.

∞

We all live with the objective of being happy; our lives are all different and yet the same.

∞

Laziness may appear attractive, but work gives satisfaction.

∞

...the final forming of a person's character lies in their own hands.

Anne Frank
b. June 12, 1929

I've always made a total effort, even when the odds seemed entirely against me.

Arnold Palmer
b. September 10, 1929

Age does not protect you from love. But love, to some extent, protects you from age.

Jeanne Moreau
b. 1929

The superior man blames himself. The inferior man blames others.

Don Shula
b. January 4, 1930

Belief in oneself is one of the most important bricks in building any successful venture.

Frank Gifford
b. August 16, 1930

Take each good day and relish each moment. Take each bad day and work to make it good.

Lisa Dado
b. 1930

If you haven't forgiven yourself something, how can you forgive others?

Dolores Huerta
b. 1930

If there's a book you really want to read but it hasn't been written yet, then you must write it.

Toni Morrison
b. February 18, 1931

There are a few times in your life when it isn't too melodramatic to say that your destiny hangs on the impression you make. Such times include the mating season and job hunting. At moments like these, you're not interested in second place.

Barbara Walters
b. September 25, 1931

I'm in motion and that's fine with me. The only thing I don't want is boredom. I don't mind being up or down, I just don't want to be still.

Lee Grant
b. October 31, 1931

The entrepreneurs know that it doesn't always work. It's not uncommon to go through a couple of failures before you hit it.

Thomas Perkins
b. March 1, 1932

What I learned led me to give so much time to Tiger (his son), and to give him the space to be himself, and not smother him with do's and don'ts.

∞

When you have to earn respect from your child, rather than demanding it because it's owed to you as a father, miracles happen.

∞

I realized that through him, the giving could take a quantum leap.

∞

Live each day to the maximum, and not worry about the future. There's only now. You must understand that time is just a linear measurement of successive increments of now. Anyplace you go on that line is now, and that's how you have to live it.

Earl Woods
b. March 5, 1932

The habit most worth cultivating is that of thinking clearly even though inspired.

Thomas H. Uzzell
b. 1932

The main reason I seek the ideas of others is for help – the diagnosis and treatment of my own isolation and the enlargement of my understanding.

Bill Moyers
b. June 5, 1933

I will die for my right to be human – just human.*

I say that if each person in this world will simply take a small piece of this huge thing, this tablecloth, bedspread, whatever, and work it regardless of the color of the yarn, we will have harmony on this planet.

Cicely Tyson
b. December 19, 1933

There is no need to fear the strong. All one needs to know is the method of overcoming them.

Yevgeny Yevtushenko
b. 1933

I don't need a man to rectify my existence. The most profound relationship we'll ever have is the one with ourselves.

The more I traveled the more I realized that our fear makes strangers of people who should be friends.

Shirley MacLaine
b. April 24, 1934

Mistakes are part of the dues one pays for a full life.

Sophia Loren
b. September 20, 1934

We all get 24 hours a day. It's the only fair thing; it's the only thing that's equal. It's up to us as to what we do with those 24 hours.

Sam Huff
b. October 4, 1934

I think we exaggerate the flexibility and freshness of young people. Advanced age can be conducive to conceptual skills that are extraordinarily important.

Ross Webber
b. 1934

New links must be forged as old ones rust.

Jane Howard
b. May 4, 1935

Your own excellence, success and greatest pride comes from only one person – you.

Frank Robinson
b. August 31, 1935

You have to leave the city of your comfort and go into the wilderness of your intuition...what you'll discover will be wonderful. What you'll discover will be yourself.

Alan Alda
b. January 28, 1936

I am telling young people that if you're dissatisfied... with the way things are, then you have got to resolve to change them.*

Barbara Jordon
b. February 21, 1936

Here is the test to find whether your mission on earth is finished: If you're alive it isn't.

Richard Bach
b. June 23, 1936

If folk can learn to be racist, then they can learn to be antiracist. If being a sexist ain't genetic, then, dad gum, people can learn about gender equality.*

Johnnetta Betsch Cole
b. October 19, 1936

If you have confidence in your idea, then do it, no matter how harsh it is. Don't give up and you will make it. That's what I experienced.

K. Philip Hwang
b. 1936

I believe that the more critical you are of your own performance, the higher standards you have, the better you become at what you do.

Don Maynard
b. January 25, 1937

Friendship is more important than money. Friendship is more important than art.

Jack Nicholson
b. April 22, 1937

My father told me, "Son, there are only six words that express what you do in business – find a need and fill it."

Pat McGovern
b. 1937

I came to understand that it was important to me to pursue those things that I cared about, and I really didn't care if people didn't like me for it.*

Maxine Waters
b. August 15, 1938

The critical responsibility for the generation you're in is, to help provide the shoulders, the direction, and the support for those generations who come behind.

Gloria Dean Randle Scott
b. 1938

The trouble with being in the rat race is that even if you win, you're still a rat.

Lilly Tomlin
b. September 1, 1939

Make sure that the career you choose is one you enjoy. If you don't enjoy what you are doing, it will be difficult to give the extra time, effort and devotion it takes to be a success.

Kathy Whitworth
b. September 27, 1939

You're never a loser until you quit trying.

Mike Ditka
b. October 18, 1939

If we didn't continue to learn, we would be in trouble.

∞

Complacency is a continuous struggle that we all have to fight.

∞

I'm a firm believer in the theory that people only do their best at things they truly enjoy. It is difficult to excel at something you don't enjoy.

Jack Nicklaus
b. January 21, 1940

If you are honest with yourself and can look into a mirror and believe that you have given one hundred percent, you should feel proud.

John Havlicek
b. April 8, 1940

We can say "Peace on Earth," we can sing about it, preach about it, or pray about it, but if we have not internalized the mythology to make it happen inside of us, then it will not be.*

Betty Shabazz
b. May 28, 1940

Sometimes it takes years to really grasp what has happened to your life.*

Wilma Rudolph
b. June 23, 1940

Everything is practice.

Pele
b. October 23, 1940

To become different from what we are. We must have some awareness of what we are.

∽

It's not daily increase but daily decrease – hack away the unessentials.

Bruce Lee
b. November 27, 1940

We encourage people to take risks and just go for it. I've always believed that people are more apt to do well than do badly.

Allen Michels
b. 1940

You don't get to choose how you're going to die, or when. You can only decide how you're going to live. Now!

Joan Baez
b. January 9, 1941

Art is the only way to run away without leaving home.

Twyla Tharp
b. July 1, 1941

I sought advice and cooperation from all those around me – but not permission.

∞

He who is not courageous enough to take risks will accomplish nothing in life.

Muhammad Ali
b. January 17, 1942

If people are informed they will do the right thing. It's when they are not informed that they become hostages to prejudice.*

Charlayne Hunter-Gault
b. February 27, 1942

Unfortunately, sometimes people don't hear you until you scream.

Stefanie Powers
b. November 12, 1942

To be somebody, a woman does not have to be more like a man, but has to more of a woman.

Sally E. Shaywitz
b. 1942

Don't compromise yourself. You are all you've got.

Janis Joplin
b. January 19, 1943

When you have confidence, you can have a lot of fun and when you have fun, you can do amazing things.

∞

To be a leader, you have to make people want to follow you, and nobody wants to follow someone who doesn't know where he's going.

Joe Namath
b. May 31, 1943

Art is not for the cultivated taste. It is to cultivate taste.

∞

Mistakes are a fact of life. It is the response to the error that counts.

Nikki Giovanni
b. June 7, 1943

One important key to success is self- confidence. An important key to self-confidence is preparation.

Arthur Ashe, Jr.
b. July 10, 1943

I have always worked in my hobby, whatever that was at the time.

George Tate
b. 1943

It's never too late – in fiction or in life – to revise.

Nancy Thayer
b. 1943

It's so clear that you have to cherish everyone.*

∞

But one day when I was sitting quiet...it came to me that feeling of being part of everything, not separate at all. I knew that if I cut a tree, my arm would bleed.

Alice Walker
b. February 9, 1944

The only time that any of us have to grow or change or feel or learn anything is in the present moment. But we're continually missing our present moments, almost willfully, by not paying attention.

Jon Kabat-Zinn
b. June 4, 1944

Character contributes to beauty.

Jacqueline Bisset
b. September 13, 1944

We should always let the childlike spirit come forth.

Rod Stewart
b. January 10, 1945

Real difficulties can be overcome, it is only the imaginary ones that are unconquerable.

Theodore N. Vail
b. July 16, 1945

If I am privileged, then I have a responsibility to pay back.*

Jewell Jackson McCabe
b. August 2, 1945

A human being's first responsibility is to shake hands with himself.

Henry Winkler
b. October 30, 1945

I think the one lesson I have learned is that there is no substitute for paying attention.

Diane Sawyer
b. December 22, 1945

The way I see it, if you want the rainbow, you gotta put up with the rain.

Dolly Parton
b. January 19, 1946

Thoughts are energy, and you can make your world or break your world by your thinking.

Susan L. Taylor
b. January 23, 1946

Reality is something you rise above.

Liza Minnelli
b. March 12, 1946

I feel the most important requirement in success is learning to overcome failure. You must learn to tolerate it, but never accept it.

Reggie Jackson
b. May 18, 1946

Just as energy begets energy, so, I have discovered, love begets love.

Tom Sullivan
b. March 27, 1947

The only thing that endures is character.

∞

I believe that the day you take complete responsibility for yourself, the day you stop making any excuses, is the day you start to the top.

O. J. Simpson
b. July 9, 1947

Compete against yourself, not others, for that is who is truly your best competition.

∞

The ultimate goal should be doing your best and enjoying it.

Peggy Fleming
b. July 27, 1948

If we live, we can dream.

George Foreman
b. January 10, 1949

Don't try to fit into a man's world. Just be yourself.

Lorraine Mecca
b. 1949

Have fun doing whatever it is that you desire to accomplish...and do it because you love it, not because it's work.

Paul Westphal
b. November 30, 1950

The thing women have got to learn is that nobody gives you power. You just have to take it.

Roseanne
b. November 3, 1952

Think not of what you did yesterday, but what you can do for yourself today.

Jerry Pate
b. September 16, 1953

My view of learning has always been that play is an important way to learn.

Trip Hawkins
b. 1953

Luck is a matter of preparation meeting opportunity.

∞

I am a product of every other black woman before me who has done or said anything worthwhile.*

∞

One of my main goals on the planet is to encourage people to empower themselves.*

∞

My philosophy is that not only are you responsible for your life, but doing the best at this moment puts you in the best place for the next moment.

Oprah Winfrey
b. January 29, 1954

You never fail until you stop trying.

Florence Griffith Joyner
b. December 21, 1954

I regret not having the time to read all the great works.

Kevin Costner
b. January 18, 1955

It is how you live that counts.

∽

If it weren't for the dark days, we wouldn't know what it is to walk in the light.

Earl Campbell
b. March 29, 1955

All pressure is self-inflicted.

Sebastain Coe
b. September 29, 1956

Someone taught me everything I know.

Ron Denning
b. May 28, 1958

The greatest education in the world is watching the masters at work.

Michael Jackson
b. August 29, 1958

Even when I went to the playground, I never picked the best players. I picked guys with less talent, but who were willing to work hard, who had the desire to be great.

Earvin "Magic" Johnson
b. August 14, 1959

Success is being able to come home, lay my head on the pillow and sleep in peace.

Herschel Walker
b. March 3, 1962

When I was growing up, she (mom) cleaned people's houses during the day and cleaned a motel at night. She also raised ten children. And people try to tell me that playing two sports is hard.

∞

If I can get a child who's in pain – physically or mentally – to smile, if I can brighten his day...That makes me feel like I've actually done something worthwhile.

Vincent "Bo" Jackson
b. November 30, 1962

Oh, I'm so inadequate – and I love myself.

Meg Ryan
b. 1962

The important thing to remember is that peace comes from within your own heart and mind, not from some outside source, and when you refuse to be disturbed by things about you, life will flood your being with dynamic energy.

∞

The difference between ordinary and extraordinary is that little extra.

∞

A true friend doesn't sympathize with your weakness; instead he helps summon your strength.

Anonymous

Every day you learn something.

∞

Heart...I think heart means a lot. It separates the great from the good players.

∞

I realize that I'm black, but I like to be viewed as a person, and that's everybody's wish.

∞

I try to be a role model for black kids, white kids, yellow kids, green kids.

∞

If I put my mind to it, I've always believed I could do anything I want.

∞

You have to expect things of yourself before you can do them.

Michael Jordan
b. February 17, 1963

If you trust your nerve as well as your skill, you're capable of a lot more than you can imagine.

Debi Thomas
b. March 25, 1967

I've always known where I wanted to go in life. I've never let anything deter me. This is my purpose. It will unfold.

∞

I've learned to trust the subconscious. My instincts have never lied to me.

∞

I like the idea of being a role model. It's an honor people took the time to help me as a kid, and they impacted my life. I want to do the same for kids.

Eldrick "Tiger" Woods
b. December 30, 1975

THE MAN IN THE GLASS

When you get what you want in your struggle for self and the world makes you king for a day.

Just go to the mirror and look at yourself and see what that man has to say.

For it isn't your father or mother or wife whose judgement you must pass.

The fellow whose verdict counts the most in your life is the one staring back from the glass.

Some people might think you're a straight shooting chum and call you a wonderful guy.

But the man in the glass says you're only a bum if you can't look him straight in the eye.

He's the fellow to please, never mind the rest for he's with you clear to the end.

And you've passed the most dangerous test if the guy in the glass is your friend.

You may fool the whole world down the pathway of years and get pats on the back as you pass.

But your final reward will be heartache and tears if you've cheated the man in the glass.

Anonymous

ACKNOWLEDGMENTS

I believe help and support from family and friends are necessary ingredients for success in life. This project would have been impossible without it.

I'd like to thank; Rick Frishman, Micheal Gallagher, Frank Gifford, Lorraine Haslee, Mel & Phyllis Levin, Diane Maki, Jenifer McFadden, Dan Poynter, Karen Shaw, Kate Siegel, Randy Waters, Susan Widick, Phyllis Diller and Billy Kidd.

Also, I would like to acknowledge 22 quotations, that are marked with an (*), from *I Dream a World: Portraits of Black Women Who Changed America*, copyright © 1989 Brian Lanker. Reprinted by permission of Stewart, Tabori & Chang, Publishers.

INDEX